Safari!

By GENE S. STUART

Photographed by GEORGE F. MOBLEY

BOTH NATIONAL GEOGRAPHIC STAFF

In an African village, Nikki Basel, 11, of Bloomingdale, Illinois, plays an instrument made from an antelope horn.

BOOKS FOR WORLD EXPLORERS
NATIONAL GEOGRAPHIC SOCIETY

Contents

Tikuna Indians in dugout canoes paddle out to welcome passengers from the World Discoverer. *The ship is anchored in the Amazon River, in South America.*

COVER: *A healer in Zimbabwe, Africa, tosses sticks called "bones" into the air. He will study them after they fall. Then he will predict Nikki's future.*

Copyright © 1982 National Geographic Society
Library of Congress CIP data: p. 104

2

What is a Safari?

COURTESY OF THE LIBRARY OF CONGRESS

On safari today, more people shoot animals with cameras than with guns.

Former President Theodore Roosevelt stands beside an elephant that he killed on safari in Africa (left). In 1909 and 1910, he and his party gathered animal specimens for a museum. They brought back many for study, including most kinds of big-game animals.

A red-footed booby peers at the camera of Michel Maquinay (right). Michel, 14, spotted the seabird while in the Galapagos Islands, off the coast of South America. "I wanted to photograph it with its beak wide open," says Michel. "After a time, it finally obliged. I'm very proud of my print." Michel lives in Bogotá, Colombia.

The year is 1900. Picture yourself on safari. You probably imagine traveling across a broad plain where herds of elephants, giraffes, and zebras graze in the distance. Your senses are alert to constant danger. Lions or leopards may pounce at any moment. The grazing animals remain calm. They have not yet picked up your scent. Carefully staying downwind, you creep nearer and nearer until you are close enough to see each animal clearly in the sight of your gun. You focus on the largest elephant, take a deep breath, and pull the trigger.

At one time, the word *safari* (suh-FAH-ree) had come to mean something like that. About a hundred years ago, when people said they were going on safari, they usually meant that they were taking a hunting trip to remote areas of Africa or other countries. By that time, it had become popular for people to travel to distant lands to hunt wild animals. The hunters took home the hides and the heads of the animals they killed as trophies.

From 1909 to 1910, after his term as President of the United States, Theodore Roosevelt went on safari to Africa. His son Kermit and a team of scientists went along. They hunted down

animals for the Smithsonian Institution, in Washington, D. C. Roosevelt's journey lasted 11 months. At times, the group included as many as 450 men. Most carried supplies. Others helped with scientific projects. They killed thousands of animals to preserve as specimens for the museum collection. The Smithsonian still displays some of these animals. Roosevelt's party also killed some big-game animals as personal trophies.

The word safari did not originally mean a hunting trip. It came from an old Arabic word meaning "journey," or "voyage." Later, the Swahili, a people of mixed black African and Arab heritage, adopted the word into their language.

Today safari has come to mean as much a sightseeing journey as a hunting trip. Joyce and Mike Basel, of Bloomingdale, Illinois, lead photographic safaris to Africa. "Most trips nowadays are not for hunting," says Mrs. Basel. "The majority of people go to look at the animals and to photograph them. Hunting safaris still exist, but many more people today go on photographic safaris." Now countries are beginning to protect their wildlife. Many have established reserves and parks where animals can live safely. Many areas restrict hunting.

"Until recently," Mrs. Basel continues, "it was unusual for children to go on our safaris. But even that seems to be changing. In South Africa, we've noticed, schools encourage children to visit local wildlife areas. A lot of children there go on 'survival safaris' during the school term. They live out in the bush and learn techniques of survival in the wild."

A modern safari can be anything from an overnight stay on a game reserve to a long voyage into a vast, uncharted wilderness. In this book, you'll share the adventures of four trips to far-off places with children of your own age. "On safari," Mrs. Basel says, "children gain an understanding of the land, the wildlife, and the other people of the world."

At home on the ocean floor

A marine iguana clings to an undersea rock off the Galapagos Islands. Marine iguanas live only in the Galapagos region. No other kind of iguana feeds on seaweed or drinks seawater.

Meeting the people and the wildlife of Africa

In a village in the African country of Zimbabwe, a woman of the Matabele tribe tells Nikki Basel and her sister Kim, 9, how to grind corn (above). "The Matabele loved the children," says Joyce Basel, the girls' mother. "They were delighted that Kim and Nikki wanted to participate."

Burchell's zebras graze among acacia trees in the African country of Botswana (left). The animals live in the Moremi Wildlife Reserve, an area protected by law.

9

Exploring a camel farm   *In the Gobi in Mongolia, Lynnie Hill, 11, of Bellevue, Washington, makes friends*

with a young camel. People of this desert region raise camels for their hair and their milk, and to carry supplies.

On their way to discovery
along the Amazon River

Heading from ship to shore, a guide named Moacir Fortes (wearing a scarf) steers an inflatable boat across the Amazon River in Brazil (above). Aboard are Sarah Prance, 14, of White Plains, New York; Mike Hill, 11, of Bellevue, Washington; and Dr. Scott Mori, a scientist at the New York Botanical Garden. Their ship, the World Discoverer, *stopped frequently along the Amazon so its passengers could visit towns and wilderness areas, and meet Indians. In Coari, in Brazil, Sarah and Mike met Amazonian children who kept birds as pets. At right, Mike laughs as a parakeet gives him a friendly nip. Mike says, "I had been making bird noises—whistling. These two birds flew over to my shoulder. One seemed to be talking back to me. The villagers were friendly. They offered us fish that they were cooking over an open fire."*

On Safari to Botswana

When members of the Basel family of Bloomingdale, Illinois, travel to Africa in search of big game, no one takes weapons. The only things they aim are binoculars and cameras. They shoot only pictures to take back as trophies.

Joyce and Mike Basel lead groups of people on safaris to visit the African bush. Their daughters Nikki, 11, and Kim, 9, often go along. "Neither of us remembers our first safari," says Kim. "Both of us were still babies when we began going to Africa." Since then, the girls have gone to Africa almost every year.

A recent African safari took Nikki, Kim, and their parents to three countries: South Africa, Botswana, and Zimbabwe. In each country, they found new excitement. "In Botswana, we saw our first leopard," says Nikki. "It hid from us in tall grass. In that part of Africa the animals don't often see people, so many are shy. But some aren't. One young lioness that was resting under a tree seemed to want to pose for our cameras. She got up and walked right in front of us when we started taking pictures."

Kim adds, "I almost laughed. But I didn't want to scare her."

"On each safari, we see something we've never seen before."
KIM BASEL

On the way to adventure, guide Dereck Joubert drives the Basel family through MalaMala (MAH-luh-MAH-luh) Game Reserve, in the Republic of South Africa (left). Family members are, from the left, Nikki, 11, Joyce, Kim, 9, and Mike. A tracker rides behind them. Using binoculars, Nikki spotted the first animal that day. "It was a bushbuck, a kind of antelope," she says. "The tracker was really something. He saw animals none of the rest of us had noticed. I don't know how he did it." The Basels live in Bloomingdale, Illinois.

Two young lions rest under a tree in the Moremi (more-RAY-mee) Wildlife Reserve, in Botswana. "We saw some mother lions with cubs," says Kim. "The mothers usually keep their babies hidden. But with the safari truck, we were able to get quite close to a few."

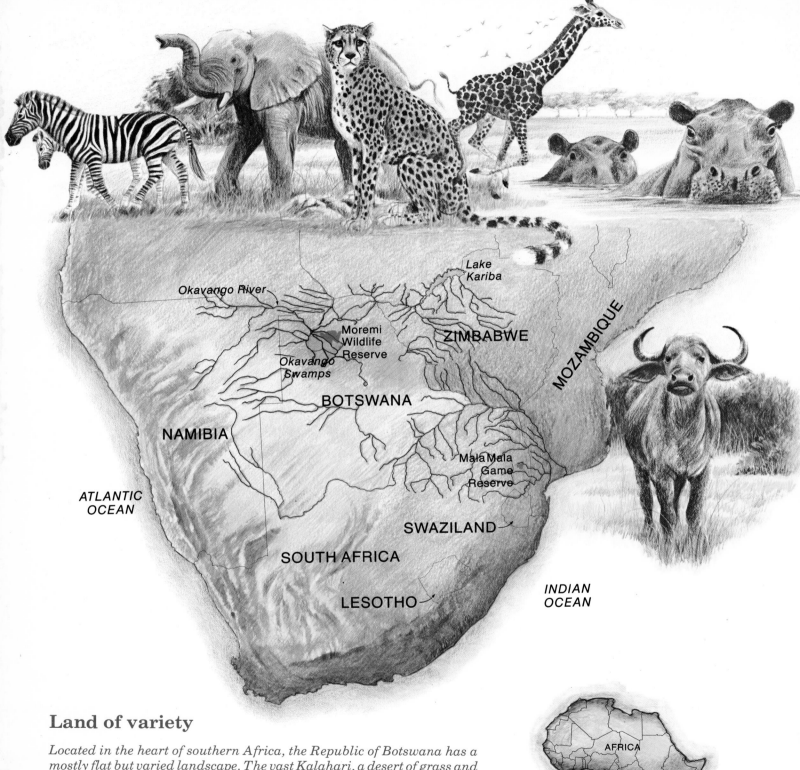

Land of variety

Located in the heart of southern Africa, the Republic of Botswana has a mostly flat but varied landscape. The vast Kalahari, a desert of grass and scrub, extends across the southern part of the country. To the north, the Okavango River drains into a basin that forms a huge swamp. Pastureland covers much of the eastern part of Botswana. Most of the country's 820,000 people live in the east. About three-quarters of the people farm or raise cattle. Others work in mines that produce diamonds, nickel, and copper.

BARBARA GIBSON

16

"Reserves are homes for animals. People are only guests."
NIKKI BASEL

Nikki follows Kim up a termite mound in Moremi. The termites build their nests of sand and earth. Some rise to 30 feet (9 m). The termites live on grass, and on a fungus that grows in the darkness inside their nest.

Not long ago, wildlife was in danger of vanishing from the area in southern Africa where the Basels travel. Herding and farming practices destroyed the animals' natural homes. Illegal hunters killed so many animals for fur, for sport, or for ivory that some species were nearing extinction. To save the animals, several countries passed laws to control hunting. People also began trying to preserve the habitats of wild animals.

The Batawana (bah-tuh-WAH-nuh), a tribe of people living in Botswana, grew concerned because hunters were killing so many animals. In 1963, the Batawana set aside 700 square miles of their own land (1,813 sq km)* to create the Moremi Wildlife Reserve. The Batawana wanted to make a refuge where animals could live safely. They also wanted to set an example for other Africans of a successful way to care for wildlife.

Moremi, now doubled in size, is part of the broad delta of the Okavango (oak-uh-VAHN-go) River. Many kinds of animals live in this area. Nikki and Kim traveled through Moremi in a safari truck. They plunged into forests and bounced across grassy plains. When they came to rivers or swamps, they traveled by boat. "The only people allowed to live in Moremi are rangers and others who protect the reserve," says Nikki. "Large settlements aren't permitted. They disturb the animals."

Governments and individuals are also working to preserve Africa's wild animals. In South Africa, where Mrs. Basel was born, a businessman named Michael Rattray set aside 125 square miles (324 sq km) of his own land as a game reserve. He named the reserve MalaMala, a local name for the rare sable antelope that lives in the area.

Whenever the Basels visited a reserve, a professional guide or a ranger traveled with them. In Moremi, their guide was Doug Skinner. "Doug knows when people should stay in their vehicle and watch animals from a distance," says Kim. "He knows when it's safe to walk along trails or to sneak up quietly on a herd of animals. He knows the areas where each kind of animal lives and where each goes for food and water. Guides have taught us a lot about wildlife."

"Sometimes life for animals in the wild seems cruel and hard to accept," Nikki says. "On safari, when I see an animal that is sick or weak, I want to help it."

"But we've learned not to interfere," Kim adds. "In nature, only the strong, healthy animals survive."

*Metric figures in this book have been rounded off.

17

**"I wanted to help it, but Dereck said,
'Do . . . not . . . touch . . . it!' "**
NIKKI BASEL

*Ranger Joubert examines a baby Cape buffalo in
MalaMala. Its mother had left it because it was
too sick or too weak to stand up. Joubert wanted to
make sure it had no disease that might spread to
other animals. "We felt sad to leave it," says Kim.
"But Dereck said it couldn't survive."*

On the alert, an adult Cape buffalo watches for signs of danger. Cape buffaloes can be fierce if they are surprised or wounded. They kill lions with their heavy horns, and they have attacked hunters. "We always watch Cape buffaloes from the truck," says Kim.

Watching animals at home in the wild

In Botswana, a sable antelope stands quietly as birds called oxpeckers examine its fur. The birds rid the animal of ticks and other pests by eating them.

As dusk settles over Moremi, a giraffe nibbles on tree leaves (left). In very dry areas, leaves are an important source of moisture.

Lifting its trunk, an elephant gets ready to powder itself with dust. "It had just come from a mud bath," says Nikki. After bathing, elephants often use their trunks to blow dirt over their wet bodies. The dirt helps protect their skin. Swaying on a tree branch, a vine snake (above) watches for prey. This snake uses venom to kill the small lizards it eats. It lives in trees and shrubs and grows to a length of 4 feet (1 1/4 m) or more.

Mike and Joyce Basel want their daughters to grow up admiring wild animals and trying to understand them. "On safari, that's what Kim and I try to do," says Nikki. "We've learned a lot just by observing."

On their latest safari, Kim and Nikki watched large numbers of zebras, giraffes, and antelopes gather at a river at dawn and drink together. They saw a herd of a hundred or more elephants feeding on treetop leaves. "Some elephants cool themselves and get rid of pesky insects by rolling in mud," Kim says. "Others suck up dust with their trunks and spray it on their backs for a nice dust bath."

The girls learned to recognize animals by the sounds they make. They learned to tell a lion's roar from that of a hippopotamus. Late at night, snorts, cracking twigs, and heavy footsteps told them a hungry hippo was nearby, looking for plants to eat.

"Sometimes you can even sense what animals might be thinking," says Nikki. "Once we saw a pack of wild dogs. They were so restless you could just feel how hungry they were. Sure enough, they soon pulled down an animal large enough to feed the whole pack."

21

"Some animals are shy, and hide; others are bold, and can be fierce!"
NIKKI BASEL

Tall grass of MalaMala couldn't hide the spotted coat of this cheetah (left). "It was resting because of the heat," says Nikki. "At first, it didn't think we had seen it. But after about a minute, it realized that we had. Then it ran away. Cheetahs are shy animals. It's rare to see one in the wild."

A baboon ignores the visitors. "We saw a lot of baboons in Moremi," says Nikki. "The mothers carry their babies piggyback. The babies are cute, and they're fun to watch." A baboon mother is a protective parent. If danger threatens, she takes her young and runs away.

"In camp, the animals are all around you."
KIM BASEL

In camp in Botswana (below), the Basels and their friends Jim and Sherry Rice, left, relax around the fire at lunchtime. Nikki helps her father put wood on the fire to make coffee and tea. Kim sits with her mother as they talk about the wild animals they saw that morning. All around their campsite, the Basels could hear animals both day and night. "Sometimes hippos came out of the river and walked right up to the tents," says Kim. "At night, you'd hear a snort, crackling leaves, then thump . . . thump . . . thump, as one walked through camp."

After going out early to observe animals in MalaMala, Nikki chats with Joubert as he cooks eggs beside the trail (left). Back in camp, the girls throw grass on a fire (below). "Every night we sat around the fire and listened to the sounds of the animals," Nikki says.

Part of the fun of a safari is living out-of-doors. In Moremi, the Basels spent their days observing animals. They slept in tents. Camping out gave them a feeling of sharing the habitat with the animals. "We often went out to look at the wildlife very early in the morning," says Mrs. Basel. "Once we accidentally woke a herd of Cape buffaloes. Then we hurried over to the water hole where the ranger thought the buffaloes would go to drink. They did go there — at least 500 of them. What a sight!"

Whenever the family cooked out on the trail, they always buried all traces of the fire and of human presence. They knew that disturbing the environment can harm the animals and spoil the beauty of the area.

After a busy day observing wildlife, the Basels enjoyed sitting around the fire in their camp. "That was when you could hear the night sounds of the animals all around you," says Mrs. Basel. "Before we turned in for the night, we'd all watch the

25

Helping the crocodile population to grow

On a crocodile farm near Victoria Falls, in Zimbabwe, Nikki holds a crocodile hatchling. She handles it carefully because even the young crocs have sharp teeth. "The skin on its back was really rough, like bark," she says. Crocodiles once were almost hunted to extinction by people who killed them for their hides. Now, farms such as this one breed the animals and release many into the wild. At right, an adult slithers out of a pond at the farm. "He looked at us as if he were thinking, 'Ah, you look good to eat!'" says Kim.

At Moremi, young crocodiles lie in the sun, with their jaws agape. Scientists think that the open mouths may help them cool off by allowing their body heat to escape into the air.

stars. In southern Africa the air is clear, and the sky seems close enough to touch. Since we were south of the Equator, we could see stars and constellations not visible in Illinois."

Snug in their tent late at night, Kim and Nikki often heard four-footed prowlers exploring the camp. But the girls were never frightened. "Once we heard something nosing around our tent window," Kim recalls. "Nikki whispered to Mom that something was sniffing us. Mom called back, 'Oh, it's just a hyena or something. Go to sleep.' We did."

Nikki and Kim never walked out of camp alone to go swimming or exploring. "There were crocodiles out there, and we knew they were dangerous," says Kim. "We kept a safe distance."

Crocodiles have played a colorful role in African history. Thousands of years ago, ancient cultures worshiped them. Egyptian priests raised crocodiles in special ponds. They believed that the animals were sacred. They decorated the animals with gold jewelry and fed them cakes, meat, and honey.

In modern times, it became fashionable to make such things as shoes and purses from crocodile hides. Hunters killed the animals by the thousand, and they became endangered. African countries later passed laws to protect them. Now, many crocodiles live on reserves. Others are raised on farms for their hides.

"We visited a crocodile farm in Zimbabwe," says Nikki. "There were crocs of all ages — from newly hatched babies to huge old ones." By law, the farm must release at least 10 percent of the ones that hatch to restock African rivers.

"Dugout canoes are river taxis."
JOYCE BASEL

Two boys who live on the banks of the Okavango River in Botswana give Nikki and Kim a ride in their dugout. The boys earn money by carrying people and goods from one riverbank to the other.

Where there are few roads in southern Africa, rivers often serve as highways. People who live along the Okavango River, in Botswana, may travel from village to village by dugout canoe. Travel by dugout takes great skill. Canoeists must steer clear of crocodiles. What looks like a bumpy island in the water may be a herd of hippos. A hippo can easily tip over a boat.

Kim and Nikki made friends with two boys who earn money by using their dugout to ferry people across portions of the Okavango. "They tried to teach us to guide the dugout with a pole," says Nikki. "But we weren't very good at it. They giggled at us. Poling takes practice. If the pole gets stuck in the muddy river bottom, you have to let go. Otherwise, the canoe may float on and leave you hanging onto your pole in the middle of the river."

Dugout canoes have many uses in the Okavango region. When villagers herd their cattle through swampy areas to cattle stations, the people ride in dugouts. People also use the canoes for fishing, an activity Kim and Nikki always enjoy on safari.

Building a dugout

For centuries, the people of the Okavango area have used dugout canoes for traveling, for fishing, and for trade. These narrow boats glide easily in shallow water and through thick reeds—places where few

BARBARA GIBSON

other craft can go. To make a dugout, a master craftsman first selects and chops down a large tree with a straight trunk. Then he shapes the trunk and hollows it out with an ax and other tools. This may take several months. Finally, he launches the canoe. Okavango dugouts vary in size. Some carry only two people; others carry more.

Spray flies as the Basels and their friends take off on a fishing trip into the swamps of the Okavango (far left). As their speedboat nears a wide pond, the girls hold on tightly, enjoying the ride. "Fishing was fun," says Nikki. "I caught a catfish that was half as long as I am."

29

Too close for comfort, *hippos move toward the edge of a pond where Kim and Nikki are standing. "They*

came right up to the bank to watch us," says Kim. "When they got too close, we started running!"

31

The hunters
and the hunted

Outside camp in Moremi, wild dogs feed on an antelope they have killed. Predators like these dogs must hunt to live. They often catch weak, old, or sick animals. Strong prey are more likely to escape.

A baby sassaby stands near its mother in another part of the reserve. Sassabies are antelopes. They have keen hearing and eyesight, which helps them detect danger. They run swiftly to escape enemies.

Discovering old tribal ways

"Blow on these bones, and I will tell your future," Nibion Ngwenya tells Nikki (left). He works as a healer among the Matabele tribe. He practices his art at the Falls Craft Village near Victoria Falls, in Zimbabwe. Visitors often come to the village to see traditional Matabele tribal life. After Nikki blows on the wooden sticks called "bones," Ngwenya throws them into the air (right). Then he studies the way the bones fall. After handling and studying other objects, he predicts the future. He told Nikki that she would marry and have five children. Kim, he said, would have three children—including twins.

In Zimbabwe, near Victoria Falls, Kim and Nikki visited the Falls Craft Village, a reconstructed Matabele village. There, people of the Matabele tribe show visitors how things were done a hundred years ago. The women make jewelry and baskets by hand. Some of the women taught Kim and Nikki to grind corn and to weave baskets. The girls also saw how a man and his three wives might have lived in the old days. Each wife would have had a hut of her own. All of the huts in Falls Craft Village are made of poles, mud, and grass. The floors are covered with a cow-manure paste that acts as floor polish.

"A traditional healer named Nibion Ngwenya still practices medicine at the village," says Nikki. "People come to him to be cured or to learn what their futures will be," Kim adds.

"His father and grandfather were healers, and he learned from them," explains Mrs. Basel. "He uses what we would call magic to cure people's ills. A special whisk made of animal hair is supposed to drive away evil spirits when he waves it in the air. He also treats people with herbs, animal bones, and magic potions. The healing profession is handed down from a parent to a favorite child." Today medically trained doctors working with healers find that many of the old cures really do help.

"Mr. Ngwenya cares about people who come to him, and he wants to help them," says Nikki. "He read Kim's and my futures by doing a lot of complicated things, including casting sticks called 'bones' on the ground. The position of the sticks after they fell told him what our futures would be. He said we'd both be healthy, and that we each would marry and have several children. He also said we would travel a lot when we grew up."

Both Kim and Nikki hope that their future travels take them back to Africa. "When we go on an African safari," Kim says, "it's like going home."

BARBARA GIBSON

Basket weaving
Practicing an age-old craft, a tribeswoman weaves a basket with a pattern of stripes. The weaver builds the basket from the bottom up. She coils a heavy reed around and around. Then she sews the coils together with thin palm leaves. Dye made from roots darkens some of the leaves.

Exploring the Galapagos

**"How beautiful
are these little babies
of the sea."**
GIGI MAQUINAY

*On Española Island, a curious sea
lion pup introduces itself to a
cautious Alexis Hunter, 8, of Santa
Barbara, California (left).
Gigi Maquinay, of Bogotá,
Colombia, prepares to take a picture
of the pair. Alexis' sister
Francesca, 14, says, "The sea lion
pups played and played. When we
left, they barked as though they
wanted us to stay."*

*Mother sea lion relaxes as she
cares for her pup on the rocky shore
of San Salvador Island (right).
"The mother was kind of sweet
looking," says Ariel Meyerowitz, 9,
of New York City. While the female,
or cow, goes fishing for food, her
mate, the bull, baby-sits.*

Have you ever dreamed of sailing far away to islands
once thought to be enchanted? Would you like to visit a wild
kingdom ruled by birds with bright blue feet, by lizards that look
like tiny dragons, and by tortoises large enough to ride? Imagine
spending a holiday exploring rocky coves and bays that pirates
once used as hideouts. Could you believe that you might see penguins living and raising their young on the Equator? Children
from four families actually experienced all of these things when
they spent a week in the Galapagos Islands, 600 miles (966 km)
off the coast of Ecuador, in South America.

They sailed aboard a ship named the *Santa Cruz.* As the ship
neared the islands, an animal welcoming committee met it.
"Dolphins escorted us," says Cindy Willetts, 11, of Weston,
Connecticut. "They were jumping out of the water and gliding
through the air. The captain slowed the ship so we wouldn't run
over them."

Guides used rubber boats to ferry the passengers from the
ship to the islands. The first stop was Española Island. There
they found sea lions, lizards, and birds. "It was a complete shock
to everyone to discover how tame the animals were," says Francesca Hunter, 14, of Santa Barbara, California. "We could walk

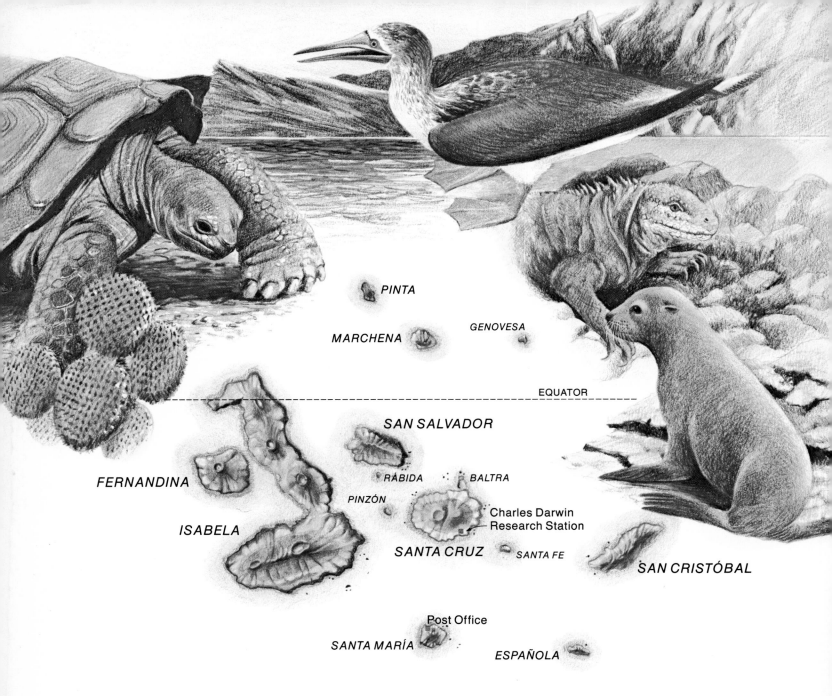

PINTA

MARCHENA

GENOVESA

EQUATOR

SAN SALVADOR

FERNANDINA

RÁBIDA

BALTRA

PINZÓN

ISABELA

Charles Darwin
Research Station

SANTA CRUZ

SANTA FE

SAN CRISTÓBAL

Post Office

SANTA MARÍA

ESPAÑOLA

Enchanted isles

*Separated from the nearest land by 600 miles (966 km)
of ocean, the Galapagos (guh-LAH-puh-gus) Islands are a
world unto themselves. Nowhere else can a visitor see
marine iguanas in the wild. Giant tortoises live there —
and only one other place on earth. Masked boobies nest
on cliffs near the shore. Sea lions, unusual sights on
tropical islands, play in cold ocean currents. Forests of
tall prickly pear cactuses grow on the crests of volcanoes.
Other areas within the islands resemble deserts. There,
the prickly pear cactuses grow close to the ground.*

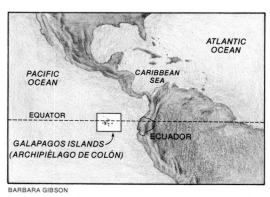

ATLANTIC
OCEAN

PACIFIC
OCEAN

CARIBBEAN
SEA

EQUATOR

GALAPAGOS ISLANDS
(ARCHIPIÉLAGO DE COLÓN)

ECUADOR

BARBARA GIBSON

Guides were always close by
and ready to share their knowledge.

On Plaza Island, off Santa Cruz, guide Polo Navarro takes his group exploring (right). At his right, Sasha Meyerowitz, 12, of New York City, discusses island wildlife with his sister, Ariel. At Navarro's left are Cindy Willetts, 11, and her mother, of Weston, Connecticut. Her father, wearing sunglasses, and Lawrence Freemon, of Tiburon, California, follow them.

A Galapagos penguin stands on the shore of Isabela Island. Galapagos penguins are the rarest penguins in the world. A few thousand live on the Galapagos Islands—and nowhere else. They are about 14 inches tall (36 cm).

close to them, and they wouldn't run away," adds Francesca's 8-year-old sister, Alexis.

Ariel Meyerowitz, 9, says, "We weren't supposed to pet the animals. Mother sea lions recognize their pups by their smell. If a pup has a human smell, the mother won't go back to it." Ariel's brother Sasha, 12, adds, "If we got too close, the big sea lions barked a warning." Ariel and Sasha live in New York City.

When the children swam or snorkeled off Española, sea lions joined in. "They were lively and playful and always ready for new pranks," says Nathalie Maquinay, 12, of Bogotá, Colombia, in South America. Nathalie's brother Michel, 14, says, "The animals seemed unafraid of humans; it was as if we were pals."

The islands and their animals have always fascinated people who visited them. Spanish explorers believed that the islands were enchanted and that they moved around in the sea. For years only pirates, whalers, traders, and a few settlers went there. Many of them hunted tortoises for food. But they left most of the other wildlife alone. "I guess that's why the animals living there now are so calm," says Francesca.

"We saw iguanas by the hundred. They were everywhere."
SASHA MEYEROWITZ

Anchored by its long claws, a lizard called a land iguana suns on a rock (left). Land iguanas live in burrows and caves. They feed on a variety of plants, including grasses and the pads and buds of the prickly pear cactus. They grow about 3 to 4 feet long (91-122 cm), and they resemble land iguanas in other parts of the world. Descendants of dogs and cats that were brought long ago as pets have killed many of the Galapagos land iguanas. "We saw more marine iguanas," says Francesca. "Masses of them covered the rocks." Like all reptiles, marine iguanas (below) have body temperatures that match the temperature around them. To warm up after feeding on seaweed in the cold ocean, they press against the sun-baked lava and absorb heat. To cool off, they rise up and catch the breeze. Cindy noticed that marine iguanas have territories. "If one iguana gets too close to another, the first one will get up on a rock and bob up and down. Then it will spit. And then it will fight."

"The booby chicks
were white and fluffy."
ALEXIS HUNTER

Thirteen main islands and many smaller ones make up the Galapagos. Many kinds of birds live on them. Some are seabirds that feed on local fish. Others, like the Galapagos albatrosses, migrate hundreds of miles each year, to South America. But they always return to the islands. Still others, such as the flightless cormorants, never leave. Over many generations, the cormorants outgrew their wings. Now the birds cannot fly at all, and can only waddle on land. But they are excellent swimmers.

Early sailors discovered some fishing birds that seemed so foolishly tame that the sailors called them *bobo,* a Spanish word for fool. In English, they became known as boobies. There are several species of boobies. Masked *(Continued on page 46)*

A family of blue-footed boobies snuggles together on the dry ground *(below)*. The blue-footed booby, like the masked booby *(upper left)*, feeds its young with fish it snatches from the sea. Boobies have a common enemy, the frigatebird. The young frigatebird at lower left will grow up to be a feathered pirate. Instead of finding its own food, it will bully another bird into dropping its catch and then steal it.

"We walked through a cactus forest."
CINDY WILLETTS

A weird forest of giant cactus plants surrounds visitors on Santa Cruz Island (right). Ariel joins Cindy and Alexis, as Francesca follows. Few kinds of trees grow on the isolated, rocky Galapagos Islands. Cactus plants thrive there. Some grow 30 feet tall (9 m). One kind of cactus, the prickly pear (bottom), has pancake-shaped leaves called pads. The pads provide iguanas and tortoises with food and moisture. During the walk, Ariel caught a glimpse of a rare vermilion flycatcher (below). "It was beautiful," she says.

44

"There were tubes
where lava once flowed."
SASHA MEYEROWITZ

A lava tube—a tunnel created by flowing lava—attracts a crowd. Visitors entered the tube through its collapsed roof. They went down the first part on a rope.

(Continued from page 42) boobies have black markings around their eyes. Red-footed boobies have bright red feet, and blue-footed boobies have blue ones.

"We saw the blue-footed boobies performing their courtship ritual," says Francesca. "The male and female hoot and put up their tails as they dance around each other. The male also whistles. When the male picks up a twig and puts it right in front of the female, it's a sign that they are going to nest. These boobies nest on the ground. We could have stepped on them if we hadn't been careful. They don't run away from people at all."

Some scientists believe the Galapagos Islands were formed millions of years ago, over a very long period of time. Hot liquid called lava poured from underwater volcanoes and from large cracks in the ocean floor. As the lava cooled, it hardened. More lava continued to bubble up, building masses of lava rock higher and higher. When the rock rose above the surface of the water, islands were born. Some of the volcanoes still erupt today, spewing out ash or lava. The children saw black lava from ancient eruptions everywhere.

On Santa María Island, the children spent the day exploring. Guides from the ship led them down a lava tube. A lava tube is a tunnel through which lava once flowed. "It was pitch black in the tube, so we carried flashlights," Cindy says. "We climbed down by rope," Alexis adds. "It was sort of scary."

Sasha remembers that, as they climbed down, the tube opened into a little funnel, like a doorway. After scrambling down a hill, the children found themselves in a big cavern.

"There was water in the cavern," says Cindy. "The bottom connects with the ocean, and it was high tide."

Francesca says, "Some people went back, but others of us kept on going. It was rocky and slippery. We were swimming, eventually. We swam pretty far. We dropped our flashlights in the water and swam in the dark. At the end we couldn't touch bottom. We dove down for the flashlights before we climbed out."

Steadied by a guide, a youngster climbs down into the lava tube (right). The entrance to the tube is steep. Then the tube gradually levels off into a gentle slope. Lava tubes are created during a volcanic eruption. A mound of lava forms and hardens on the surface. Inside the mound, molten rock continues to push up and flow downhill. Eventually, the molten rock drains out, leaving a tube. "We climbed down the tube until we reached a pool of seawater. The tube runs downhill until it joins the sea," says Nathalie Maquinay, 12.

"At Santa Cruz Island, there were huge tortoises, and the warden let me pet one. Its skin felt wrinkly and cold."

ALEXIS HUNTER

Cindy and Alexis make friends with a tortoise at Charles Darwin Research Station. Ariel and Sasha take pictures. "The tortoises were the only animals we were allowed to pet," says Francesca, at right.

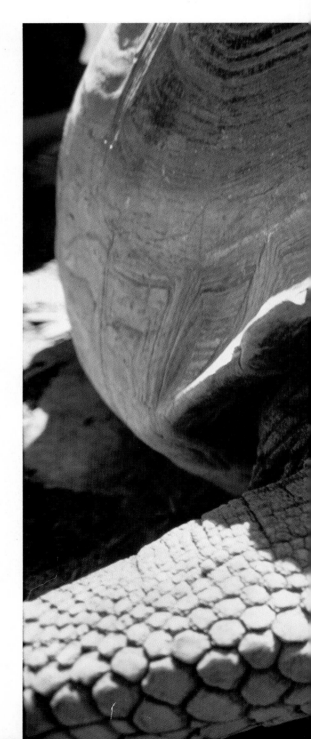

Gentle giant, a Galapagos tortoise peers from its shell (below). The shell measures about 5 feet long (1¹/₂ m). "They told me the tortoises weigh several hundred pounds," says Francesca. "One stepped on my foot, and it was heavy," adds Sasha. The tortoises can crawl about 4 miles (6 km) in a day.

The Galapagos Islands are named for the giant tortoises that live there. *Galápagos* is the Spanish word for tortoises. Today the tortoise population numbers in the thousands. Once, many more of these slow-moving animals inhabited the islands. People killed great numbers of them for food. Settlers introduced new animals—goats, dogs, cats, rats, and pigs. These animals destroy tortoise eggs and hatchlings, and plants the tortoises eat. Some kinds of Galapagos tortoises became extinct.

Now, on Santa Cruz Island, National Park wardens and scientists at the Charles Darwin Research Station are helping to increase the number of tortoises by hatching and raising the young until they are big enough to live on their own. "We saw a tortoise nursery there," says Cindy. "It was like a little town. The small tortoises had houses with grass around them." Park wardens let the young tortoises go free after about four years.

A few old tortoises live at the station, too. "They all seemed to want attention," Francesca says. "The old tortoises were the only animals the wardens let us touch anywhere in the islands."

Tiny tortoise

At birth, a Galapagos tortoise weighs less than a quarter of a pound (113 g). Female tortoises lay from 7 to 20 eggs in a hole in the dirt. The mothers cover their nests with soil, then leave. Heat from the sun-warmed soil helps the eggs develop. After three months—or as long as eight in cool climates—the babies hatch. They dig their way out of the nest with their sharp claws.

BARBARA GIBSON

"What a beautiful view we had from here."
MICHEL MAQUINAY

Bare-branched trees line the way for the Maquinay family on Isabela, the island of the Galapagos that rises highest above the sea (left). Following their father are Michel, first, then Nathalie, and then Gigi. White bark gives the trees a ghostly look. It is the season for them to shed their leaves. The Galapagos has two distinct seasons. From January through April is the rainy season. Hurricanes may also occur. For the rest of the year, the weather is dry. On Santa María Island, Cindy visits the mailbox (below). About

200 years ago, whalers on long voyages began using this spot as a post office. Ships heading home would pick up any mail left there and deliver it to its destination. Crewmen added the signs carrying the names of their ships.

51

Galapagos crab called a Sally Light-foot brightens a rock. "Sally Light-foots cover every nook and cranny of the rocks," says Sasha. These crabs stay close to the water, but they seldom enter it.

When the English naturalist Charles Darwin visited the Galapagos in 1835 to study the environment, the plants and animals he found there amazed him. He called the Galapagos "a little world within itself."

Nearly 150 years after Darwin's visit, the children on the ship *Santa Cruz* had similar thoughts. "It was like a dream." Francesca says, "I could have been on another planet. The animals weren't at all like the animals at home."

How did life in the islands become so different? Scientists believe that the ancestors of these animals and plants came from other lands long ago. Seeds floated in or were carried by winds or by birds. Animals probably swam, floated, or flew to the Galapagos. Over many centuries, these plants and animals changed slowly from generation to generation, adjusting to their new homes. Eventually, the new kinds of plants and animals had become quite different from their ancestors. This is why much of the wildlife may appear strange to most visitors to the islands.

Isabela Island lies on the Equator.

Jagged cliffs of Isabela Island rise from Pacific waters (above). Scientists think that the Galapagos Islands have existed for about three million years. Volcanic

eruptions and lava flows continue to build and change them. Six separate volcanoes eventually flowed together to form Isabela. Volcanoes still erupt there. Today the island is 80 miles long (129 km). When hot lava spills down the side of a volcano, it kills the plants and the animals in its path. The Equator crosses Isabela where the cliff rises at the left.

Varieties of finches

Thirteen species of finches live in the Galapagos Islands. Their bills vary in shape. Finches that probe for insects in decayed wood have long, sturdy bills. Those that pick tiny insects off leaves have small, slender bills. Those that crack seeds have heavy bills. Scientists think that all these finches had a common ancestor.

BARBARA GIBSON

"Sitting close to the water was a flightless cormorant."
FRANCESCA HUNTER

Cooling off, a Galapagos flightless cormorant stretches its wings. When the first cormorants arrived on the islands long ago, they probably had strong wings and could fly as other cormorants do. But on the islands, the birds had no enemies, and their need to fly was reduced. Eventually, the cormorants became larger than their ancestors had been. Their wings did not keep pace, so the birds lost their ability to fly.

54

Using sea urchin spines, Cindy forms her name on a beach of Española. "We were ready to leave, but the wardens waited for me to finish," she says. "I'm sure the sand has covered it by now."

The Galapagos is the only place in the world where huge lizards called iguanas swim underwater and eat ocean plants. It is the only place on the Equator where penguins live. Most penguins live in cooler regions. But because cold ocean currents sweep past the Galapagos, these flightless birds are comfortable there. Rats and bats are the only land mammals native to the Galapagos. There are no freshwater animals such as frogs or salamanders. But there are grasshoppers that cannot fly. Some species of butterflies and moths there are midget-size.

Many visitors find the plants as strange as the animals. In places where plenty of rain falls, forests of plants similar to sunflowers grow 30 to 40 feet tall (9-12 m)—three times as tall as true sunflowers. In drier places, prickly pear cactuses have strange red bark and may grow 30 feet tall (9 m). All other varieties of prickly pears grow small and close to the ground.

The South American country of Ecuador owns the Galapagos Islands. The Ecuadorean government became concerned about visitors destroying the wildlife there. In 1959, Ecuador made the islands a national park. Also in 1959, the Darwin Foundation set up a research station in the islands for scientific study and nature protection. Various other countries are also involved in the conservation effort.

Now all visitors must register with the National Park Service. They can visit only certain sites, and they must take along a certified naturalist guide. Galapagos guides, called wardens, teach visitors how to preserve the Galapagos. "The wardens taught us not to take any objects, such as shells, rocks, or plants back with us," Cindy says. "They explained that, if we did, we could permanently disturb the environment." Government officials want to make sure that future visitors will always be able to see the islands in their natural, undisturbed state.

Acrobat with flippers swims near San Salvador Island (left). "The seals swam right up to us," says Sasha. "They weren't afraid of us at all. They acted as though we were just other seals. They would zoom up, look into our masks, then zoom away."

Legend has it that pirates who once used San Salvador Island as a hiding place may even have buried loot on its shores. The children found no trace of pirate treasure, but they did find adventure. When they dove into a rocky inlet on the island's edge, they discovered that they were swimming with seals.

Francesca's greatest pleasure in the Galapagos was sharing their animal kingdom. "We were in their world. They weren't in ours at all," she says. "It was very enjoyable. If I could do anything I wanted, I would go back to the Galapagos."

For the Maquinay family, the trip had a special meaning. Robert Maquinay, father of Gigi, Michel, and Nathalie, says, "The Galapagos Islands are part of our own South American Continent. We expected to find a new, different, and fascinating aspect of nature. This proved to be true. Our visit left in each of us a lasting experience combining fun and education."

world are the animals this tame."
FRANCESCA HUNTER

"I was resting on a rock after swimming with the seals when I heard a seal behind me. I turned around and extended my hand in friendship," Cindy recalls (right). Below, passengers from the ship swim in a natural pool surrounded by rocks. Their friends watch from a rock bridge. Water flows under it and joins the sea.

Journey to Mongolia

*Exploring the ancient city of
Samarkand, Tony Rossabi, 10, and
his mother peer through stone
latticework (left). They are looking
into a courtyard off the Registan,
the main square at the center of the
city. "We saw old buildings
covered with blue and yellow tiles,"
Tony recalls. Samarkand is in
Uzbekistan, part of the Union of
Soviet Socialist Republics. The
Rossabis live in New York City.*

*Americans in Western dress
mingle with women of Samarkand
in brightly colored dresses (right).
Lynnie Hill, 11, of Bellevue,
Washington, wears a cowboy hat.
Her mother, in dark glasses, follows
her. Tony's sister, Amy, 14, walks
close to a wall of Shah-i-Zinda,
a group of tiled mosques (MOSKS)
and tombs built in the city between
the 11th and 15th centuries.*

For centuries, merchants made their way back and
forth overland between Asia and Europe. Merchants heading
from China to Europe and the Middle East carried in their packs
valuable silks, spices, perfumes, and other items prized in the
West. Merchants heading east toward China and India took
horses, wines, linen and cotton fabrics, gold, glass, and other
goods desired by people of the Far East. The journey was long
and dangerous. The routes crossed mountains and deserts. For
protection against bandits and against the forces of nature, the
merchants traveled together in caravans.

The paths the merchants followed are known as trade routes.
The trade routes that linked China and India to Europe and the
Middle East came to be called the Silk Road. Samarkand, in

central Asia, was one of its most important trading centers. In the main square of the city, called the Registan, the merchants could buy or trade luxuries from all over the known world.

Visitors still pass through Samarkand, but journeys that once took months, or even years, can now be made in a few days from almost anywhere in the world. Recently, 14-year-old Amy Rossabi, her brother, Tony, 10, and their parents arrived from New York City. With them were Lynnie Hill, 11, and her mother, of Bellevue, Washington. Like the merchants of old, the families stopped in Samarkand. They were on their way to Mongolia.

Samarkand is one of the oldest cities in central Asia. It has a long history filled with adventure. The city was founded more than 2,500 years ago. It has changed hands many times. Alexander the Great conquered it in 328 B.C. The Mongol emperor Genghis Khan, called Chinggis by the Mongolians, seized it in 1220. The ruler Timur, also called Tamerlane, held the city from 1369 to 1405. He made Samarkand the capital of a new empire.

Amy, Tony, and Lynnie visited Shah-i-Zinda, an area of the city holy to Muslims. It is a place of old tombs and of Muslim temples called mosques. Delicate tilework covers many of the buildings. Shah-i-Zinda, or Living King, was a cousin of the Muslim Prophet Muhammad. Muslims believe he is buried here.

Lynnie remembers the central Asian women she saw praying in the mosques. "Their silk dresses are so colorful they stand out like trees in the middle of the road," she says. A series of stone steps leads up to the narrow, twisting passageways of Shah-i-Zinda. As the children entered and left the area, they counted the steps very carefully. "If you get the same number both times, you're considered a good person. If you get a different number, then you're considered a sinner," says Lynnie. "There are 36 steps. I got the same number going up and coming down."

Merchants still come to Samarkand to sell their goods in the busy marketplace. "It's like a bazaar," Amy says. "There are little stands that sell food—mostly fruit and vegetables. The goods vary from a type of flat bread to peppers and grapes." Melon salesmen willingly posed before Amy's camera. When Amy gave them Polaroid pictures of themselves, the men presented her with melons in return.

"The people of Samarkand were nice and very friendly," says Lynnie. But Samarkand was just one of many stops for the Americans. So, like members of an ancient caravan, the children gathered their packs and continued on their journey across central Asia to Mongolia.

Mongolia nestles between giant neighbors, China and the U.S.S.R.

BARBARA GIBSON

Along the Silk Road

In a bazaar in ancient Samarkand, a silk merchant shows off his goods. Silk was first produced in China. It was one of many items traded along the Asian caravan routes later known as the Silk Road. Samarkand was one of the major trading centers of the Silk Road.

Amy holds a melon as Lynnie kneels down for a closer look at the mounds of fruit for sale in a bazaar in Samarkand (right). "The melons were sweet and juicy," says Lynnie.

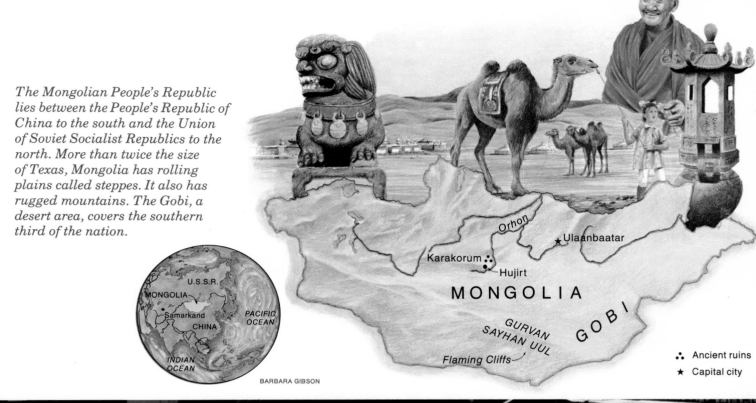

The Mongolian People's Republic lies between the People's Republic of China to the south and the Union of Soviet Socialist Republics to the north. More than twice the size of Texas, Mongolia has rolling plains called steppes. It also has rugged mountains. The Gobi, a desert area, covers the southern third of the nation.

Orhon

★ Ulaanbaatar

Karakorum ⋰

Hujirt

MONGOLIA

GURVAN
SAYHAN UUL

GOBI

Flaming Cliffs

U.S.S.R.

MONGOLIA

Samarkand

CHINA

PACIFIC
OCEAN

INDIAN
OCEAN

BARBARA GIBSON

⋰ Ancient ruins

★ Capital city

"From the top of a hill, we saw a whole community of gers."
TONY ROSSABI

On the outskirts of Ulaanbaatar, the capital of Mongolia, tent dwellings called gers (GAIRS), or yurts, cover part of a valley. Most citizens of Ulaanbaatar now live in modern apartments. But people in this neighborhood still use one-room gers. The tents are made of felt and canvas stretched over wooden frames, and they can be moved from place to place.

Outside Gandan Monastery, the Buddhist center in Mongolia, Tony and Amy reach up to touch the smoke of incense burning in a metal urn. Worshipers traditionally drop an offering in this urn before entering the temple.

A Buddhist monk carries a hat made of dyed camel's hair. Once, many of the men of Mongolia chose to spend their lives in monasteries. Monastery life is less popular now.

The Mongolian People's Republic is a young nation. It won its independence from China only about 60 years ago. But Mongolia has a long history. Centuries ago, many tribes of wandering nomads shared the land. Then one tribe, the Mongols, united all the other tribes. The leader of the Mongols at that time was Genghis Khan. His armies then set out to conquer other lands. Under his grandson Kublai, the Mongol empire reached its peak. It stretched from the Pacific Ocean across most of continental Asia to the Danube River in Europe, and to the Persian Gulf in the Middle East.

Although it is much smaller than the old empire, Mongolia today covers an area more than twice the size of Texas. About half of all Mongolians live in towns and in modern cities.

Amy, Tony, and Lynnie saw both the new and the old. One of their favorite places was the historic Gandan Monastery, in Ulaanbaatar, the capital. There Mongolia's few remaining Buddhist monks live and worship. "We watched the ceremonies of the monks and heard their chants," Lynnie says. "They sat on wooden benches with bowls of fermented mare's milk before them. They drank some milk, prayed, drank again, and chanted."

"Seeing the statue reminded me of my German shepherd."
LYNNIE HILL

A fierce stone lion on the grounds of Bogdo Gegen Palace doesn't scare Lynnie (above). In fact, Lynnie growls right back. Buddhists believe creatures like this ward off evil spirits. Ignoring the guardian gods painted on the main entrance to the palace, Lynnie hangs on the sturdy metal door handles (right). Now a museum, this palace was built for Bogdo Gegen. He was the last Buddhist political leader of Mongolia. He died in 1924. Today visitors to the palace see a collection of Buddhist art and items that belonged to Bogdo Gegen.

A Buddhist monastery now stands near the site of Genghis Khan's capital city.

Gentle hills surround the walls of Erdene Dzuu, once a busy Buddhist monastery (below). Now the buildings house a museum. Some of them have been restored. "Each temple is filled to the brim with statues of Buddha and his followers," Amy says. Begun in 1586, the monastery once was home to 10,000 monks. Along the monastery wall stand 108 pointed memorial towers called stupas (STOO-puhs). They honor important Buddhist holy persons of the 16th and 17th centuries.

COLLECTION OF THE NATIONAL PALACE MUSEUM, TAIPEI, TAIWAN, REPUBLIC OF CHINA

Genghis Khan
More than seven centuries ago, Mongol leader Genghis Khan founded one of the largest empires the world has known.

Lynnie rides a stone tortoise as Amy adjusts her camera (above). This creature is one of the few original objects that remain of Karakorum, the capital of Genghis Khan's empire. In 1388, Chinese invaders destroyed the city. Bricks from it helped build Erdene Dzuu, seen behind the girls.

Tony and Lynnie share a Polaroid photograph with a Mongolian girl at Erdene Dzuu (right). She holds a balloon they gave her. The American visitors made friends with many Mongolian children.

66

"Gers are homey, roomy, comfortable, and warm. We hope to get one!"
LYNNIE HILL

Inside a brightly decorated ger, Lynnie stretches out on her bed while Amy rests on a painted wooden dresser. The girls spent several nights in ger camps similar to this one for tourists in Hujirt. Even in August, the Mongolian nights can be chilly. But the ger stayed snug. "A wood-burning stove kept the ger warm," Lynnie reports. "One of my favorite things was having a fire at night. We'd bring bread back from dinner and toast it on top of the stove."

Round white tents called *gers* or *yurts* have served as homes for Mongolian nomads for centuries. "Most Mongolians who live outside cities still use them," Lynnie says. "The herders move about with their animals during the summer, but they stay in one place during the winter." When they decide to move, they take down the family ger. They can do it in about an hour. Then they pack the ger on camels or in carts and move it to another place. They set the ger up just as quickly as they took it down. The walls are made of wooden slats fastened together so they fold, like the safety gates used for babies. Canvas and felt cover the outside. Gers are sturdy. They do not blow down in windstorms. In winter, temperatures may fall to -50°F (-46°C). When that happens, Mongolians add several layers of felt to the tent cover. Even in a blizzard, ger dwellers stay warm and cozy.

The visitors spent several days in guest ger camps. "Each ger has a stove," Amy says. "We burned wood at night to keep warm."

One ger was fit for a king. Lynnie says, "In Bogdo Gegen Palace, in Ulaanbaatar, we saw the winter ger of the last Buddhist ruler of Mongolia. It had a leopard-skin cover trimmed with purple ribbons. The furniture and ceiling supports were inlaid with gold. My mom and I like gers so much we hope to get one to set up in our yard at home."

Lynnie, her mother, and other tour members walk around a ger camp in the Gobi, a desert region. Heavy ropes hold down the canvas covers of the round tents to keep them from blowing away in high winds.

At a Mongolian-style picnic beside the Orhon River, the children shared part of their lunch with unexpected visitors. "There were birds flying around that looked like hawks," says Tony. "We threw some meat up, and they caught it in the air."

"Some caught the meat with their beaks, some with their claws," Lynnie says. "The birds were really scary. They waited until the meat was almost on our heads, then they swooped down at us. They screamed as they swooped. They were like dive-bombers. We ducked quickly."

When people think of a desert caravan, they usually picture a string of camels crossing a hot, sandy wasteland. Amy, Tony, and Lynnie traveled into an area of dry plains called the Gobi. Instead of riding camels, they climbed aboard a bus for a bumpy ride. And instead of a hot, sandy wasteland, they found a rocky plain, streams, coarse grass, mountains, and very cold weather. But the Gobi is still a true desert because it has little rainfall.

In a rocky field beside the Orhon River, the tour group pauses for a picnic. "The river was narrow, but the current was fast," Lynnie recalls. "Our guide told us it was much too dangerous for swimming."

"Lunch was shish kebabs made with yak meat."
AMY ROSSABI

Amy, Tony, and Lynnie dig into a meal of yak-meat shish kebabs washed down with mineral water. "Yak tastes like steak," Lynnie reports. This picnic took place near Yol Canyon. "We found a deep valley filled with flowers," Amy says. "We saw some mountain sheep there, too. They were beautiful with their full coats and curved horns."

Sandy fun   *"We rolled and slid down the dunes," says Tony. Most of the Gobi is a dry, rocky plain covered with*

coarse grass and shrubs. But Amy, Lynnie, and Tony visited one spot that had soft sand dunes just right for sliding. 73

"We took a bumpy ride to look for bones."
TONY ROSSABI

With the help of a Mongolian friend, Lynnie digs in the Gobi for dinosaur bones as her mother watches. Many fossils have been found in the Gobi. Scientists have reconstructed complete skeletons from their finds here. They also have unearthed dinosaur eggs. Lynnie, Amy, and Tony dug where their guide suggested. But they turned up only a few bones from a sheep, a yak, or a horse—not from a dinosaur.

Searching for dinosaur eggs, Tony kicks at a ridge of dry earth (right). In this part of the Gobi, sometimes called the Flaming Cliffs, many dinosaur fossils have been found.

BARBARA GIBSON

Finding dinosaur eggs in the Gobi

About 60 years ago, an expedition led by American scientist Roy Chapman Andrews made an exciting discovery near the Flaming Cliffs. Expedition members found dinosaur eggs. Until that time, no one had known that dinosaurs laid eggs. The 9-inch-long (23-cm) eggs were laid by a species of dinosaur named Protoceratops. An adult grew to a length of 9 feet (3 m). It might have looked like the drawing above. The Andrews expedition found hundreds of other fossils. Scientists are still uncovering the remains of animals that inhabited the Gobi millions of years ago.

75

Meeting the wildlife of the desert.

Mongolian horses graze and frisk on a rolling hillside in the Gobi (left). Almost everyone in Mongolia rides these sturdy horses. Even small children take part in races designed to test how fast their horses can gallop.

In the Gurvan Sayhan Uul, a trio of mountain peaks in the Gobi, Tony, Lynnie, and Lynnie's mother hiked deep into Yol Canyon. "We saw huge rock walls, a waterfall, and a stream," says Tony. "Walking along the stream, we saw more hawklike birds, and wild gerbils."

"When the birds came," Lynnie says, "a gerbil would whistle a signal. The other gerbils would run across the desert and go into a little cave one by one."

"The gerbils warned each other," Lynnie's mother explains. "Little shrill whistles shot down the canyon as the shadows of the birds passed over. In the United States, gerbils are popular pets. I didn't know they had relatives on the Mongolian desert."

Tony walks ahead during a hike through Yol Canyon, in the Gobi. Lynnie and her mother follow (above). During the walk, they saw wild gerbils, relatives of the pets many Americans keep in their homes. "We saw about 25 of them," Tony says.

Camels have carried people across the desert for centuries.

Making friends with children in Mongolia was fun for Tony, Amy, and Lynnie. Since the children there speak Mongolian, the official language, or Russian, communicating was a little difficult. Most of the time, the Americans talked to their new friends in sign language. They played games. "We played volleyball, ball toss, and hide-and-seek," Tony says. "We also taught the Mongolians to play with a Frisbee."

Mongolian children play hundreds of games using knucklebones of small animals. Some of the games resemble marbles, jacks, checkers, and dice. Mongolians also enjoy sports. One of the most popular is wrestling. Mongolian boys dream of winning a national wrestling championship.

Mongolians celebrate Independence Day on July 11. Then, children and adults compete in wrestling and archery matches, and in horse races. Children 6 to 12 race small, shaggy Mongolian horses on courses 16 or 31 miles long (25 or 50 km).

While in Mongolia, the young travelers visited a farm near Hujirt. They rode horses and learned to milk cows. They also visited a camel farm in the Gobi. "The people raise camels for their hair, for their milk, and to use as pack animals," says Amy.

"Camel's milk is frothy, like a milkshake," Lynnie says. "But it tasted awful to me. It's bitter. Mare's milk isn't too terrific, either. It tastes like dusty yogurt."

At the camel farm, the children went for a camel ride. When a handler tapped the camels with a stick, they knelt down and the children climbed aboard. Camels in Mongolia have two humps. "You sit between the humps," Lynnie says. "When camels walk, you go up and down and sideways, and up and down and around."

Riding a camel was a new experience for everyone. Discovering new things was what they enjoyed most about their safari. "Everything was different—the place, the people," Lynnie says. "The food really was different. I'd never tasted yak. Mare's milk will never be my favorite drink. But just having the chance to taste it was an experience I'll remember for a long time."

Camel caravan crosses the Gobi with Tony, Amy, and Lynnie on board (right). "Camels give very bumpy rides," Lynnie says. "But you're not likely to fall off unless you fall sideways." After the ride, the three Americans were offered food—including camel's milk—in the herder's ger. Mongolians raise camels for their hair and their milk.

On a camel farm in the Gobi, a young Mongolian girl leads a two-humped camel (right). Dusk outlines other camels (far right). These camels, known as Bactrians (BACK-tree-unz), live only in central Asia. One-humped, or Arabian, camels live in warmer desert areas.

Voyage up the Amazon

"Hang on, Mom!" As Mike Hill, 11, dips his hat into the water, his mother keeps a firm hold on his shirttail (left). Mike was fishing for crayfish. His mother is Dr. Byrde Hill. Sarah Prance, 14, laughs at his efforts. Mike, of Bellevue, Washington, and Sarah, of White Plains, New York, had just begun a voyage that would introduce them to life in the world's largest rain forest. "My mom agreed to let me fish for piranhas," Mike says. "But she didn't want me to become bait." Piranhas (pih-RON-yuz) are small meat-eating fish with jaws full of razor-sharp teeth.

A baby sloth dangles from a leafy branch. Dr. Ghillean Prance, Sarah's father, climbed up a tree and cut off a branch with this sloth attached. Then he climbed back to ground level so Mike and Sarah could examine the animal. This kind of sloth is a slow-moving mammal that spends almost all of its life in trees. It grows about 25 inches long (64 cm). After Sarah and Mike had looked the sloth over, Dr. Prance put it on a bush where it could climb back into the trees.

Every passenger had boarded the seagoing ship *World Discoverer*. The loud, deep-pitched horn blasted a goodbye. The big ship let loose its lines and moved slowly out of the port of Belém, Brazil. But the *World Discoverer* did not sail into the ocean. Instead, it began a 15-day journey up the broad Amazon River. Mike Hill, 11, of Bellevue, Washington, and Sarah Prance, 14, of White Plains, New York, were passengers on the *World Discoverer*. They were off on a South American river safari.

Mike's voyage was a birthday gift from his mother, Dr. Byrde Hill. She had promised to take him on a fishing trip. "She didn't expect to end up fishing in the Amazon!" Mike says. Sarah's trip was a homecoming journey to Brazil with her father, Dr. Ghillean Prance. Sarah and her family had lived in Manaus, Brazil, for a total of six years while Dr. Prance studied Amazonian plants. "I had never traveled the length of the river," she says. "I had only seen parts of it. I wanted to go far up the river, to see wildlife, and to visit Indian tribes."

Mike's and Sarah's adventure took them more than 2,000

From beginning to end, the Amazon flows for 4,000 miles.

Amazon explorers peer from an inflatable boat called a Zodiac (left). They are looking for caimans. Caimans (KAY-muns) are reptiles that resemble alligators.

From its starting point high in the Andes range in Peru to its wide mouth on the Atlantic coast of Brazil, the Amazon River flows 4,000 miles (6,400 km). The area around the river is called the Amazon basin (below). This basin drains about one-third of the South American Continent. The world's largest rain forest grows within the basin. Plants and animals in great variety live there. On their safari, Sarah and Mike rode the Amazon through parts of three countries — Brazil, Colombia, and Peru.

BARBARA GIBSON

miles (3,200 km) up the Amazon. They traveled across Brazil, along the southern tip of Colombia, and into Peru. Their safari ended at Iquitos, Peru. Beyond Iquitos, the Amazon is too shallow for large ships to navigate.

The Amazon is the longest river in the Western Hemisphere. It flows for 4,000 miles (6,400 km) from beginning to end. In length, it is second only to the Nile River, in Africa.

The Amazon begins in Peru, as a tiny stream high in the Andes mountain range. As it flows toward the Atlantic Ocean, heavy rains and hundreds of smaller streams and rivers, called tributaries, feed water into it. Rivers of several different colors flow into the Amazon. Some have water colored brown by silt washed down from the Andes. Others have water tinted black by decaying vegetation. Still others have water that sand has filtered clear. These rivers reflect the blue sky. "The Amazon itself is the color of coffee with cream," says Sarah.

The largest rain forest in the world borders the Amazon. More kinds of plants and animals live in this rain forest than in any other place on earth. Some of the trees grow as tall as 15-story buildings. More than 3,000 kinds of butterflies flit through the forest. More kinds of fish live in the Amazon and its tributaries than in any other river system in the world.

SOUTH AMERICA

COLOMBIA

Bora and Witoto Villages
Ilha do Aranapu
Napo
Negro
EQUATOR
ATLANTIC OCEAN
Iquitos
Vendaval
Leticia
Coari
Manaus
AMAZON
Ilha do Careiro
Alter do Chão
Pará
Belém
PERU
Ucayali
Madeira
Tapajós
ANDES
BRAZIL

PACIFIC OCEAN
Source of the Amazon

As the *World Discoverer* cruised up the Amazon, it made frequent stops. At each stop, the ship lowered small craft called launches, or inflatable boats named Zodiacs. Passengers boarded them to visit coastal towns, to observe jungle wildlife, and to go fishing. Sarah and Mike caught several fish. Mike was proudest of his piranhas. Mike says, "You just bait a hook with a piece of raw beef and drop it in. The piranhas go 'chomp,' and you've got a fight. They're strong little things. I hooked ten piranhas, but four got away. I'm sure they were the biggest."

While fishing near an island named Ilha do Careiro, Mike and Sarah saw squirrel monkeys swinging through the trees. Caimans—reptiles that resemble alligators—floated among reeds near the shore. Dr. Hill says, "Our guide gently lifted up some of the young caimans with an oar for the kids to see."

"They were about three feet long," says Sarah. "I've been out with my father at night to look for caimans. When light from our flashlights hits them, their eyes glow red."

On the Rio Tapajós, a blue-water tributary of the Amazon, the passengers rode to a sandy beach. There, the ship's crew set up barbecue grills made out of split oil drums. When children from the nearby village of Alter do Chão appeared, they were invited to the cookout. "As the evening grew dark, we all sat around a bonfire and began singing folk songs," Mike says. "Everybody joined in. The children didn't know the words, but they quickly learned the tunes and sang anyway. Other visitors who go back there just may hear kids humming 'Oh! Susanna.' "

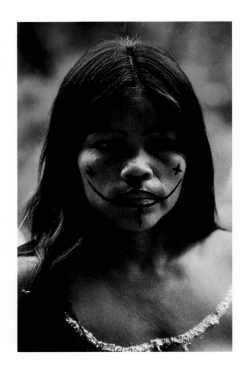

Ready for a tribal dance, a Witoto Indian wears delicately drawn makeup. Today many Amazonian Indians put on traditional costumes and makeup only for special occasions. They wear Western clothing the rest of the time.

84

"I brought the jaws back as a souvenir."
MIKE HILL

"I felt as if I were pulling in the shark from the movie Jaws," Mike says. What he caught was a 7-inch (18-cm) piranha (above). "Piranhas really put up a fight," he says. Here, he shows off the sharp teeth of his catch. He took the piranha's jaws home as a souvenir. During his safari, Mike learned that piranhas are seldom as vicious as most people think. Usually, they become dangerous to humans only when they are trapped in shallow pools and cannot find enough to eat. A young spectacled caiman (left) appeared by the riverbank while Mike and Sarah were exploring a river inlet on Ilha do Careiro.

At home on the river

Two Amazonian boys go fishing in a rainwater lake near Manaus, in Brazil (below). One of the young fishermen holds a long spear and a short canoe paddle. Grass pokes up through the water. This area is a lake only during the rainy season. The rest of the time it is a pasture.

Surf's up! Children race to their dugout canoes (left). They are rushing to ride the waves that the World Discoverer *makes as it passes by. This house, along the Breves Channel in Brazil, rests on stilts. At flood time, usually in late May, the river rises to floor level — sometimes higher. Tall açaí (ah-sah-EE) palm trees surround the house. Sarah says that the açaí palm fruit makes a good, dark-purple ice cream.*

Amazonian children use the Amazon and nearby rivers in many ways. Some paddle to and from school in dugout canoes. For fun, many swim or fish. And for some youngsters and their families, home is a house floating on a river.

In Manaus, a local guide named Moacir Fortes used his own dugout to take Sarah and Mike visiting. "Moacir grew up in Manaus," says Sarah. "He took us to meet his friends who live in a floating village on the Rio Negro, a black-water river. The houses are built on rafts made of tree trunks. When the river rises and falls, the houses go up and down with it." The visitors bought bread at a floating bakery. They even saw a floating gas station.

Mike and Sarah saw another way that people use the rivers. "Often, when our ship passed, children were let out of school," Mike says. "All the kids jumped into their dugouts and came out to ride the waves the ship made. Sometimes even grown-ups stopped work to join in. It's the local roller coaster!"

"They all liked the frankfurters."
MIKE HILL

World Discoverer *cookout on a beach near the village of*

Alter do Chão, in Brazil, attracts local children. The passengers invited the youngsters to eat with them.

"The parrot was trained to sit on a broomstick and twirl around like a gymnast."
MIKE HILL

While visiting children in a floating village near Manaus, Mike gets acquainted with a pet parrot (above). "It perched on my finger. Then it walked up my arm and across my shoulders," Mike recalls. At first, Mike wanted to take home a macaw, like the one at left. "Then I decided I'd rather take pictures of macaws flying in the jungle than have one taken from the wild," he says. Later, Mike learned that it is illegal to take macaws out of Brazil.

Eating candy that Sarah gave them, Tikuna Indian children walk down a path in the village of Vendaval, in Brazil (below). They are going to see another boatload of passengers arrive. The people of Vendaval build their houses off the ground to keep animals out and for ventilation. The stilts also keep the homes from flooding during cloudbursts.

Touch of color   Heliconia, *a flowering plant, attracts Mike and Sarah as they make their way through undergrowth*

Layers of life

From the air, the Amazon rain forest looks like a solid sea of green. But from the ground, the rain forest proves to be not one world but many. The forest separates into several different layers. The tallest trees tower above the rest of the forest. Their tops form the emergent layer. Here, brightly colored birds fly freely. Beneath this layer is the canopy, formed by slightly shorter trees. Here, monkeys leap and chatter. Still shorter trees make up a third level, called the lower story. It's darker here, because the upper levels block out much of the light. Vines twist and tangle among the branches. Sloths pass through here on their regular journeys from the canopy to the ground. At ground level, the rain forest is dark and shadowy. Little light reaches the ground and fewer plants grow.

The world's largest ants live in the Amazon rain forest. Their scientific name is Dinoponera gigantea. *The female is more than an inch long (2¹/₂ cm). Below, a winged male watches as a female twice his size carries a cocoon. Females have powerful jaws and stingers. They gather the food and fight to defend the colony.*

BARBARA GIBSON (BOTH)

on Ilha do Aranapu, an island in the Amazon.

With the help of Captain Heinz Aye, Sarah learns to use the World Discoverer's *sextant. Navigators use sextants to help them calculate the position of their ships. The ship also has radar and sonar.*

"Small channels can change very, very quickly."
SARAH PRANCE

The *World Discoverer* is like a floating town. It has a library, a movie theater, a gym, and a swimming pool on board. It also serves as a classroom—a place to learn about the people, the plants, and the animals of the rain forest.

Sarah's father told the passengers many interesting things about people, plants, and insects. Other scientists on board were experts on birds and other animals. "Way out in the middle of nowhere, you could ask any question about the Amazon and get a good answer," says Mike. "Each night before dinner we talked about everything we'd seen that day."

A special treat was a tour of the ship with the captain, Heinz Aye. Mike and Sarah even visited the engine room and the galley, or kitchen. Captain Aye commands the ship from an area called the bridge. There, he showed Sarah and Mike the instruments he uses to guide the ship through shallow channels.

"At one place, a big freighter was grounded in a shallow channel," says Sarah. "That happened because mud and sand had blocked the channel. Small channels can change very, very quickly." Sometimes the *World Discoverer* crew had to search for new passages that the ship could go through. Once Captain Aye and some crew members took Sarah and Mike with them in the launch when they went to look for a passage. The group explored and mapped a new, deep channel. "We took the map back to the ship so the captain could set a new course," says Sarah. "The map was only good for a little while, though. In a few weeks, a channel can change. The next ship may have to find a new route."

"Channels are named for the ship that discovers them," Mike says. "We helped find the World Discoverer Channel."

Where the Rio Tapajós joins the Amazon, passengers ride in a launch lowered from the World Discoverer. Many large and small rivers, called tributaries, join the Amazon along its route to the sea. The Amazon system carries more fresh water than any other river system on earth.

Where the waters meet *Like a huge, slithery snake, a stream flows into the Tapajós near the*

spot where it joins the Amazon. There are a few sandy beaches along the Amazon, but most of the banks are muddy.

"The people bring in their goods by canoe."
SARAH PRANCE

Dugout canoes jam the Amazon riverbank at Leticia, in Colombia. Boats such as these bring fresh produce to market. The Amazon region produces many kinds of fruit—especially bananas—as well as vegetables, meat, and fish. Some merchants sell their goods right from their boats. Others take them to a marketplace on shore. "Some of the sellers come from far away," Sarah says. For the long trip to market, people often attach outboard motors to their boats.

Mike bargains with a young merchant in a market in Manaus (below). "I bought a bag of green tomatoes because the boy was such a hard worker," says Mike. In this market, Mike also bought a wire fish trap and the bow and arrows he's holding under his arm. At this stall, he paid cash for his purchases. At other stops, Mike and Sarah traded fishhooks and colored marking pens for locally made souvenirs.

"Marmosets have manes and faces like tiny lions."
SARAH PRANCE

Pygmy marmoset nestles in the palm of Sarah's hand (left). Sarah met this monkey, the smallest kind in the world, in the Tikuna village of Vendaval. A Bora Indian girl cradles a pet margay kitten, a kind of wild jungle cat (below). "Indian children along the Amazon keep a lot of different animals as pets," Sarah says. "Some girls carry marmosets in their hair."

In Brazil near the Colombian border, Mike and Sarah visited their first Indian village. Vendaval is a village of Tikuna Indians. It sits on a cliff high above the Amazon River. Mike and Sarah traded goods with the Tikuna. They exchanged flashlights, T-shirts, and colored marking pens for woven bags, bowls, paddles, and spears. "The Indians were very friendly," says Sarah. "Most of the Tikuna in the village now speak Portuguese, the language of Brazil, instead of their native language. They wear Western clothes. But many of them still file their teeth to sharp points. It's an old tradition."

In Peru, near Iquitos, Sarah and Mike visited Witoto and Bora Indian villages. "The villages are next to each other, but the people speak different languages," says Sarah. The Witoto invited their visitors to take part in a dance traditionally performed before a hunt. "It began as a simple dance," says Sarah, "but then it got fast and ended with everyone running in and out of the meeting hut."

Flying home to Washington, Mike thought about his journey. "The whole trip was overwhelming," he says. "There's nothing that can ever compare with it. But one thing concerns me. I'm afraid that the areas we visited may not stay the same much longer. On some parts of the river we noticed oil slicks. And along many of the banks, settlers and developers had cut down trees. You could see roads stretching back into the forest. I don't think the Amazon rain forest will totally disappear. It's too big. But in parts of the world, wilderness is just going to disappear.

"Some places will hold out. Some people value their wilderness too much to destroy it. I'm all for that."

At a village near Iquitos, in Peru, a Bora Indian woman decorates Sarah's face with traditional designs (right). "Seeing the Indian tribes made the biggest impression on me during the trip," Sarah says. In each of their villages, the Bora and the Witoto tribes danced for the World Discoverer *passengers.*

Index

Bold type refers to illustrations; regular type refers to text.

Consultants

Joyce and Mike Basel, Fun Safaris Inc.; Stephen A. Halkovic, Jr., Director, Research Institute for Inner Asian Studies, Indiana University; John G. Hangin, Department of Uralic and Altaic Studies, Indiana University; Loren McIntyre; Ghillean T. Prance, New York Botanical Garden; Morris Rossabi, Case Western Reserve University — *Chief Consultants*

Glenn O. Blough, LL. D., University of Maryland; Patricia Leadbetter King, National Cathedral School; Violet Tibbetts — *Educational Consultants*

Nicholas J. Long, Ph.D. — *Consulting Psychologist*

The Special Publications and School Services Division is grateful to the individuals, organizations, and agencies named or quoted within the text and the individuals cited here for their generous assistance:

Daryl Boness, National Zoological Park; Elmer R. Broxson, Georgetown University; Theodore R. Dudley, National Arboretum; Tim Farrell, MalaMala Game Reserve; Thomas H. Fritts, U. S. Fish and Wildlife Service; William Harbaugh, University of Virginia; Judith M. Hobart; Nicholas Hotton III, Smithsonian Institution; Devra G. Kleiman, Karl R. Kranz, Dale L. Marcellini, National Zoological Park; Scott A. Mori, New York Botanical Garden; Tjako S. Mpulabusi; James N. Norris, Smithsonian Institution; James K. Russell; Joseph Segars, U. S. Department of State; Thomas E. Simkin, Smithsonian Institution; Doug Skinner, Moremi Safaris; Paul Slud, Smithsonian Institution; T. C. Swartz, Society Expeditions Cruises, Inc.; Bruce M. Shwedick, Reptile World, Inc.; Richard W. Thorington, Jr., Smithsonian Institution; George E. Watson, Smithsonian Institution; Ralph M. Wetzel, University of Connecticut; William A. Xanten, National Zoological Park; Paul A. Zahl.

map 38; name 48; national park 48, 55; research station 48; seasons 51; settlers 39, 48; volcanoes 46, 52-53
Game reserves 6, 17, 27; *see also* MalaMala Game Reserve; Moremi Wildlife Reserve
Gandan Monastery, Mongolia **63**
Genghis Khan 60, 63; portrait **66**
Gerbils: pet 77; wild 77
Gers (tents) **62-63, 68-69**
Giraffes **20**, 21
Gobi (desert), Asia **10-11**, 61, **69-79**
Guides **12**, 36, **39**, 46, **47**, 55, 74; *see also* Rangers; Trackers; Wardens

Healers: Africa **34, 35, cover**
Heliconia **92**
Hippopotamuses 21, 24, 28, **30-31**
Horses 58; Mongolian: **76**, 78
Houses **86**, 87, **90-91**; *see also* Gers
Hunting 4, 6; collecting museum specimens 4, 6; laws restricting 6, 17; trophies **4**, 6

Iguanas *see* Land iguanas; Marine iguanas
Indians of South America *see* Bora; Tikuna; Witoto
Isabela Island, Galapagos Islands **39, 50-53;** size 53

Kalahari (desert), Botswana-Namibia-Republic of South Africa 16
Karakorum (ruins), Mongolia 66

Land iguanas **40-41**, 44
Lava: flows 53; tubes **46-47**
Leticia, Colombia **98-99**
Lions 14, 15, 21; statue **64**
Lizards 21, 46; *see also* Iguanas

Macaws 90
MalaMala Game Reserve, South Africa 14, 17, **18-19, 22-23, 25**
Manaus, Brazil 87, 90, **99**
Marine iguanas **6-7**, 38, 41, 55
Markets **61, 98-99;** ancient 60
Marmoset, pygmy **100**

Masked boobies 38, **42**, 46
Matabele tribe, Africa **9, 34, 35, cover**
Milk: camel's 11, 78; mare's 63, 78
Monasteries, Buddhist 63, **66-67**
Mongol Empire 63, 66
Mongolian People's Republic **10-11, 62-79;** capital 63; desert *see* Gobi; food 63, **70-71**, 78; history 63; horses 58, **76**; housing *see* Gers; map 61; sports 77, 78
Moremi Wildlife Reserve, Botswana **8-9, 15**, 17, **20**, 25
Mosques: Samarkand, U.S.S.R. **59**

National parks 6; Ecuador 48, 55
Negro, Rio, Brazil 87, **90**

Okavango River, Africa 17, **28-29**; map 16
Orellana, Francisco de 84
Orhon River, Mongolia **70**
Oxpeckers **21**

Parakeet 12, **13**
Parrots **90**; *see also* Macaws
Penguins 36, **39**, 55
Peru 100, **101;** map 83
Pets **13**, 44, 77, **90, 100**
Photography *see* Cameras
Piranhas 80, 84, **85**
Plaza Island, Galapagos **39**
Prickly pear cactuses 38, 41, **44**, 55
Protoceratops **75**

Rain forest, Amazon River region 80, 83, **92-93;** layers of life **93**
Rangers: Africa 17, 25
Red-footed boobies **5**, 46
Republic of South Africa *see* South Africa, Republic of
Roosevelt, Theodore **4**, 6

Sable antelopes 17, 21
Safaris: photographic safaris 6; word meaning 4, 6
Sally Light-foots (crabs) **52**
Samarkand, U.S.S.R. **58-61**
San Salvador Island, Galapagos Islands **37**, **56, 57**
Santa Cruz Island, Galapagos Islands **44-45**, 48

Santa Cruz (ship) 36, 52
Santa María Island, Galapagos Islands **46-47;** mailbox **51**
Sassabies: baby and mother **33**
Scientists 4, 6, **12**, 48, 74, 75
Sea lions 38, **39**; pups **36, 37**
Seals: Galapagos Islands **56**
Shah-i-Zinda (Muslim shrine), Samarkand, U.S.S.R. **59**, 60
Silk Road 58; bazaar along **60**
Sloths **93**; baby **81**
Snakes *see* Vine snake
South Africa, Republic of 6, 14
Stupas **66;** defined 66
Swimming 46, **56-57**

Tapajós, Rio, Brazil 84, **94-97**
Temples *see* Monasteries; Mosques
Termite mound **17**
Tikuna Indians **2-3**, **91**, 100
Tortoises 36, **38**, 39, 44, **48-49;** stone tortoise **66**
Trackers, safari 14

Ulaanbaatar, Mongolia **62-63**
Union of Soviet Socialist Republics *see* Samarkand, U.S.S.R.

Vendaval, Brazil **90-91**, 100
Vermilion flycatcher **44**
Vine snake **21**
Volcanoes 38, 46, 52-53; *see also* Lava

Wardens 48, 55
Wild dogs 21, **32-33**
Wilderness areas *see* Game reserves, National parks; *see also* Amazon River region
Wildlife *see* Animals; Game reserves
Witoto Indians **84**, 100

Yaks: bones 74; yak meat **70-71**
Yol Canyon, Mongolia **70-71**, 77
Yurts *see* Gers

Zebras 21; *see also* Burchell's zebras
Zimbabwe, Africa **9**, 14, **26-27, 34, 35, cover;** map 16

Additional Reading

Readers may want to check the two-volume *National Geographic Index* in a school or public library for related articles and to refer to these National Geographic Society books: *Book of Mammals*, Vol. I & II; *Lost Empires, Living Tribes.* The following books also are suggested for supplementary reading. (An A in parentheses after the listing indicates a book for advanced readers.)

Botswana: Arundel, Jocelyn, *The Wildlife of Africa.* N.Y.: Hastings House, 1965. Beebe, B. F., *African Lions and Cats.* N.Y.: David McKay, 1969. Carr, Archie, *The Land and Wildlife of Africa.* Alexandria, Virginia: Time-Life Books, 1964. (A). Couffer, Jack and Mike, *African Summer.* N.Y.: G. P. Putnam's Sons, 1976. D'Amato, Janet and Alex, *African Crafts for You to Make.* N.Y.: Julian Messner, 1969. Douglas-Hamilton, Iain and Oria, *Among the Elephants.* N.Y.: Viking Press, 1975. Johnson, Peter and Anthony Bannister, *Okavango, Sea of Land, Land of Water.* Cape Town: C. Struik, 1977. (A). Larson, Thomas J., *Tales from the Okavango.* Cape Town: Howard Timmins, 1972.

Galapagos: Darwin, Charles, *The Voyage of the Beagle.* N.Y.: Doubleday and Co., 1962. (A). Dawson, E. Yale, *A Brief Natural History of the Galapagos Islands for Young People.* Washington, D.C.: Organization of American States, 1971. Moore, Tui DeRoy, *Galapagos, Islands Lost in Time.* N.Y.: Viking Press, 1980. (A). Selsam, Millicent E., *Land of the Giant Tortoise.* N.Y.: Four Winds Press, 1977. Thornton, Ian, *Darwin's Islands, A Natural History of the Galapagos.* N.Y.: Doubleday and Co., 1971. (A).

Mongolia: Spuler, Bertold, *History of the Mongols.* Berkeley: University of California Press, 1971. (A). Stein, Aurel, *On Ancient Central-Asian Tracks.* Chicago: University of Chicago Press, 1974. (A). Yapp, Malcolm, *Chingis Khan and the Mongol Empire.* St. Paul, Minnesota: Greenhaven Press, 1980.

Amazon: Ayensu, Edward S., editor, *Jungles.* N.Y.: Crown Publishing Co., Inc., 1980. (A). Batten, Mary, *The Tropical Forest: Ants, Ants, Animals and Plants.* N.Y.: Harper & Row, Inc., 1973. Prance, Ghillean T. and Anne, *The Amazon Forest and River.* Woodbury, N.Y.: Barron's Educational Series, Inc., 1982. (A). Sterling, Tom, *The Amazon.* Alexandria, Virginia: Time-Life Books, 1973. (A).

Library of Congress CIP Data
Main entry under title:
Stuart, Gene S.
    Safari!
    (Books for world explorers)
    Bibliography p.
    Includes index.
    SUMMARY: Describes the experiences of travelers on safaris to areas in southern Africa, Mongolia, the Galapagos Islands, and along the Amazon River, and their observations of local customs, animal and plant life, and geography. Includes a wall poster, games, and puzzles.
    1. Safaris—Juvenile literature. [1. Safaris. 2. Voyages and travels. 3. Adventure and adventurers. 4. Animals] I. Mobley, George F., ill. II. Title. III. Series.
G516.S88   910.4   80-8799
ISBN 0-87044-385-2 (regular binding)   AACR2
ISBN 0-87044-390-9 (library binding)

Composition for SAFARI! by National Geographic's Photographic Services, Carl M. Shrader, Chief; Lawrence F. Ludwig, Assistant Chief. Printed and bound by Holladay-Tyler Printing Corp., Rockville, Md. Color separations by the Lanman-Progressive Corp., Washington, D. C.; and Lincoln Graphics, Inc., Cherry Hill, N.J. FAR-OUT FUN! printed by Federated Lithographers and Printers, Inc., Providence, R.I.

Safari!
By Gene S. Stuart
Photographed by George F. Mobley

PUBLISHED BY
THE NATIONAL GEOGRAPHIC SOCIETY
WASHINGTON, D. C.

Gilbert M. Grosvenor, *President*
Melvin M. Payne, *Chairman of the Board*
Owen R. Anderson, *Executive Vice President*
Robert L. Breeden, *Vice President,*
    Publications and Educational Media

PREPARED BY THE SPECIAL PUBLICATIONS
AND SCHOOL SERVICES DIVISION

Donald J. Crump, *Director*
Philip B. Silcott, *Associate Director*
William L. Allen, William R. Gray, *Assistant Directors*

BOOKS FOR WORLD EXPLORERS
    Ralph Gray, *Editor*
    Pat Robbins, *Managing Editor*
    Ursula Perrin Vosseler, *Art Director*

STAFF FOR THIS BOOK
    Margaret McKelway, *Managing Editor*
    Thomas B. Powell III, *Picture Editor*
    Ursula Perrin Vosseler, *Designer*
    Donna B. Kerfoot, Suzanne Nave Patrick,
    Patricia Rosenborg, *Researchers*
    Jacqueline Geschickter, Catherine O'Neill,
    Judith E. Rinard, *Legend Writers*
    Mary Elizabeth Davis, *Editorial Assistant*
    Artemis S. Lampathakis, *Illustrations Assistant*
    Mary Jane Gore, *Art Secretary*
    John D. Garst, Jr., Patricia K. Cantlay, Gary M. Johnson, Joseph Ochlak, *Map Production*

STAFF FOR FAR-OUT FUN!
    Patricia N. Holland, *Project Editor;* Roger B. Hirschland, *Text Editor;* Peter J. Balch (page 3), Susanah B. Brown (page 20), Dru Colbert (pages 17-18), Roz Schanzer (pages 1-2, 4-8, 11-13, 15-16, 19), *Artists;* Patricia K. Cantlay, *Mechanicals;* Glover S. Johns III, *Photography Consultant.* Computer program by James B. Caffrey and Joe Fowler

ENGRAVING, PRINTING, AND PRODUCT MANUFACTURE
    Robert W. Messer, *Manager;* George V. White, *Production Manager;* Mark R. Dunlevy, *Production Project Manager;* Richard A. McClure, Raja D. Murshed, David V. Showers, Gregory Storer, *Assistant Production Managers;* Katherine H. Donohue, *Senior Production Assistant;* Katherine R. Leitch, *Production Staff Assistant*

STAFF ASSISTANTS: Nancy F. Berry, Pamela A. Black, Nettie Burke, Claire M. Doig, Rosamund Garner, Victoria D. Garrett, Jane R. Halpin, Nancy J. Harvey, Sheryl A. Hoey, Joan Hurst, Virginia A. McCoy, Merrick P. Murdock, Cleo Petroff, Victoria I. Piscopo, Tammy Presley, Carol A. Rocheleau, Katheryn M. Slocum, Jenny Takacs

MARKET RESEARCH: Mark W. Brown, Marjorie E. Hofman, Meg McElligott

INDEX: Colleen Brown DiPaul